UNDERSTANDING APPLE INTELLIGENCE 2024

A Revolutionary Personal Intelligence System And How You Can Leverage Apple Intelligence

Jeremy Severn

TABLE OF CONTENTS

Chapter One: Introduction to Apple Intelligence

With the release of Apple Intelligence, users may now access highly relevant and practical personal intelligence data through the use of generative models. This innovative solution combines the power of Apple silicon with personal context to speed and simplify daily chores.

Apple Intelligence, the personal intelligence system for iPhone, iPad, and Mac, uses generative models and personal context to deliver relevant and useful intelligent information to users.

On June 10, 2024, Apple Intelligence—a personal intelligence system for iPhone, iPad, and Mac—was launched. It combines the strength of generative models with unique context to provide highly valuable and relevant intelligence. iOS 18, iPadOS 18, and macOS Sequoia all demonstrate how deeply

Apple Intelligence is integrated. It leverages the power of Apple hardware to perform activities across apps, comprehend and generate language and graphics, and take advantage of contextual information to streamline and expedite daily tasks. Apple sets a new norm for privacy in AI with Private Cloud Compute, allowing for the expansion and flexing of compute power between on-device processing and larger, server-based models that run on dedicated Apple silicon servers.

We are thrilled to introduce a new era of Apple innovation. Apple CEO Tim Cook said, "Apple Intelligence will change what users can do with our products and what our products can do for our users." "We're excited for people to see what AI is capable of since only Apple can deliver it. Our innovative method delivers genuinely useful intelligence by fusing generative AI with the individual context of the user.

Additionally, it can access that data in a way that is totally secure and private, enabling users to accomplish the tasks that are most important to them."

Apple has unveiled Apple Intelligence, a cutting-edge personal intelligence system that combines the power of Apple silicon with generative models to deliver incredibly relevant and useful intelligence to consumers. This innovative solution speeds up and simplifies daily tasks.

Apple Intelligence sets a new standard for AI privacy with its deep integration into iOS 18, iPadOS 18, and macOS Sequoia. The company ensures that customer data is never stored or made public using Private Cloud Compute, and third-party experts can review the code running on Apple silicon servers to verify privacy.

Among the system's many intriguing characteristics are:

- Writing Tools: a feature available across the entire system that promotes better writing and user communication.
- Image Playground: a creative and exciting way to quickly make images.
- Genmoji is a creative way to express yourself through the production of original emojis.
- With Memories, users may create the story they want to see by adding a description.
- Siri: has enhanced language comprehension skills, a stronger integration with the system, and the ability to expedite and streamline daily tasks.

Furthermore, Apple Intelligence integrates ChatGPT access into every Apple platform so that customers can take advantage of its expertise without hopping between products.

With Apple Intelligence, the company has raised the bar for AI innovation and privacy once again. This revolutionary personal intelligence system is anticipated to fundamentally alter how individuals use their devices and gather information.

Chapter Two: Writing Tools/Resources

Writing Tools, a system-wide tool that enhances writing and promotes more effective communication, is one of the many amazing features offered by Apple Intelligence. Users may use Writing Tools practically anywhere they write to edit, proofread, and summarize content.

- **<u>Innovative Skills for Language Production and Interpretation</u>**

With the all-new system-wide Writing Tools included in Mail, Notes, Pages, and third-party apps, users can edit, proofread, and summarize content almost anywhere they write on iOS 18, iPadOS 18, and macOS Sequoia. With Apple Intelligence, people may write better and communicate more successfully in new and creative ways.

Writing Tools help users feel more confident in their writing, whether they are creating the perfect email, organizing their class notes, or proofreading a blog post. Apple Intelligence's Rewrite feature allows users to choose from several drafts of their writing and adjust the tone to suit the intended readership and task.

Rewrite helps create the perfect words for any given situation, whether it's putting the finishing touches on a cover letter or adding some fun and originality to a party invitation. It checks for errors in grammar, sentence structure, and sentence structure; additionally, it makes change suggestions and justifies them so users can review and approve them.

Summarize allows users to select text to be summarized as a list, table, bulleted list, or easily readable paragraph.

A user selects Proofread or Rewrite from the Writing Tools menu while working on an email.
A user opens the Notes app and chooses the Summarize option in order to compile their notes regarding holistic health.

Users may practically everywhere they write edit, proofread, and summarize information thanks to systemwide writing tools provided by Apple Intelligence.

With Summarize, users can select which content to have condensed into a list, table, paragraph, or bulleted list of essential elements.

With Mail, staying on top of emails has never been easier. Priority Messages lets you see the most important emails at the front of your inbox, like airline tickets or dinner invitations that are due that same day. Rather than seeing a preview of the first few words of every email in your inbox, users can view summaries without ever opening the message.

To browse lengthy threads, simply tap on relevant details. Smart Reply will identify questions and provide suggestions for a timely response to ensure that all concerns are addressed in an email.

To guarantee that every issue is handled in an email, Smart Reply will identify inquiries and provide recommendations for a timely reply.

A strong command of the language also extends to notifications: Priority Notifications rise to the top of the stack to highlight the most relevant information; Reduce Interruptions is a new Focus that only shows alerts that would require quick attention, such as a text about an early daycare pickup, in order to help users stay focused on what they're doing. Summaries help users quickly scan lengthy or stacked notifications to display crucial information directly on the Lock Screen, such as when a group conversation is especially active.

The new focus, Reduce Interruptions, only shows alerts that could need an immediate response.

The Notes and Phone apps now allow users to record, transcribe, and summarize audio. When a recording begins during a call, participants are notified instantly, and Apple Intelligence generates a summary at the end of the session to help participants remember key information.

Chapter Three: The Visual Diary (Image playground)

With three styles accessible for users to develop images: Sketch, Illustration, and Animation, Image Playground offers a creative and enjoyable way to quickly create graphics. It's easy to use and can be integrated into programs like Messages.

With Image Playground, self-expression and communication are considerably more pleasant.

People can express themselves and communicate in new ways thanks to the creative picture creation capabilities enabled by Apple Intelligence. Users can quickly create humorous graphics with Image Playground by choosing one of three styles: animation, illustration, or sketch. Image Playground is easy to use and easily integrated into many apps, like Messages. It can also be found in a specific app, which is perfect for experimenting with different concepts and aesthetics. Since each image is created on the device, users can experiment with as many images as they like.

iPad Pro showing off the new Image Playground app.

Users can create funny images quickly and effortlessly with Image Playground, which is directly incorporated into apps like Messages.

With Image Playground, users may make an image by providing a description, add a person from their own photo collection to the image, choose their favorite style, and choose from a number of concepts from categories like locales, costumes, accessories, and themes.

- **Establishing Visual Playgrounds**

With Image Playground, users may access a wide range of concepts from categories like themes, costumes, accessories, and destinations.

With the Messages Image Playground experience, users can quickly create humorous photos for their friends. They can also receive personalized suggested themes related to their conversations. To make image creation even more efficient and relevant, for example, while a user is texting a group about hiking, they will see suggested concepts related to their friends, their destination, and their activity.

Users can utilize Image Playground to quickly create humorous graphics for their friends and receive personalized suggestions for themes related to their talks in Messages.

To enhance the visual appeal of notes, users can use the new Image Wand in the Apple Pencil tool palette to access the Image Playground in Notes. Rough sketches can be turned into charming images, and users can even select blank spaces and use the surrounding context to construct an image. Third-party applications that make use of the new

Image Playground API, along with applications such as Keynote, Freeform, and Pages, are compatible with Image Playground.

The Image Wand in the Apple Pencil tool palette allows users to create images by highlighting parts that are blank and use the surrounding context.

Chapter Four: Genmojis

Genmoji is a new way to express oneself through the production of original emojis. Users may create Genmoji of themselves and their loved ones based on photographs by just typing a description into a Genmoji maker.

- **<u>Designing Emojis for Any Circumstance</u>**

People can express themselves with original Genmojis, which take emoji to a whole new level. To see a user's Genmoji and other options, type in their description. Moreover, users can use their photos to create Genmoji of friends and family. Like emoji, Genmoji can be used as a reaction in a Tapback, shared as a sticker, or used inline with messages

.

The instruction "Smiley relaxing wearing cucumbers" that the user receives determines the Genmoji they should select.

Users have the option to choose a person from their photo collection and create a Genmoji that looks like them.

With the New Photo Features, Users Now Have Greater Control

The ability to precisely search for images and videos is made possible by Apple Intelligence. For example, viewers can access specific segments of videos by using search terms like "Maya skateboarding in a tie-dye shirt" or "Katie with stickers on her face." Additionally, the new Clean Up tool can identify and remove distracting background elements from photos without inadvertently altering the image's focus.

- **<u>Equipment for Image Cleaning</u>**

You can find and remove distracting background elements from images without accidentally affecting the subject matter by using images' new Clean Up feature.

Memories lets users create a story they want to watch by simply typing in a description; Apple Intelligence will then use that description to pick the best photos and videos, write a screenplay with chapters based on themes identified in the photos, and use language and image recognition to arrange those photos into a movie with a clear storyline.

Apple Music will also suggest music based on the user's memories. User photos and videos remain private on the device and are not shared with Apple or anyone else, just like with all other Apple Intelligence services.

Three iPhone 15 Pro screens show the Memory Movie making procedure.

Memories enables Apple Intelligence to choose the best photos and videos, make a storyline, and arrange everything into a movie with a clear narrative based on a user's description.

Chapter Five: Memories - Reliving the Moment, Rekindling the Emotion

Simply put a description into Memories, and Apple Intelligence will choose the best photos and videos based on the description, weaving language and image recognition together to create a story that the user wants to see.

Memories are the threads that weave our past, present, and future together. They are the moments that make us laugh, cry, and feel alive. But, how often do we struggle to recall the details of a cherished memory? How often do we wish we could relive that moment, rekindle that emotion? Apple Intelligence's Memories feature makes that possible.

Imagine having a personal historian that captures your memories, preserves them, and presents them in a way that transports you back to that moment. That's what Memories does. It's an AI-powered feature that curates your photos, videos, and audio recordings, and weaves them into a narrative that's both personal and poignant.

With Memories, you can create movies from your favorite moments. Want to relive your wedding day? Memories will create a beautiful film that captures the joy, laughter, and tears. Want to remember your child's first birthday? Memories will craft a heartwarming movie that highlights the milestones and memories.

But, Memories is more than just a movie maker. It's an experience that evokes emotions, sparks nostalgia, and fosters connection. It's a way to share your stories, your legacy, with loved ones. Imagine watching a movie of your family's history, narrated by your grandmother's voice, or seeing a slideshow of your childhood, set to music that transport you back to that era.

Memories also allows you to search for specific moments, using natural language. Want to find all the photos of your cat, Mr. Whiskers? Simply type "Mr. Whiskers" and Memories will surface all the relevant images. Want to relive your European vacation? Type "Europe trip" and Memories will take you on a visual journey through your travels.

The beauty of Memories lies in its ability to capture the essence of a moment, without the need for tedious editing or curating. It's an AI-powered feature that understands the context, emotion, and significance of each memory, and presents it in a way that's both personal and impactful.

In a world where memories are fleeting, Apple Intelligence's Memories feature is a game-changer. It's a way to hold onto the past, cherish the present, and create a legacy for the future. As we continue to navigate the digital landscape, it's clear that

Memories will play a significant role in shaping our relationship with technology, and with each other.

Chapter Six: Siri

Siri is a more useful tool now that it has deeper system integration, improved language comprehension, and the ability to automate and accelerate everyday tasks. Users can type to Siri and switch between text and speech to interact with her in whatever way feels suitable at the moment.

- ## Siri's New Era

A sophisticated glowing light surrounds the edge of the screen when Siri is in use, adding to the app's all-new appearance. With the aid of Apple Intelligence, Siri's integration with the system is strengthened. Siri may expedite and simplify daily tasks and is more natural, contextually relevant, and personal due to its enhanced language understanding skills. It can keep up with users who mispronounce words and carry over context from one request to the next. Additionally, users can converse with Siri in whatever way feels appropriate at the moment by typing to her and alternating between speech and text.

A user is typing to Siri on the iPhone 15 Pro.
Now, users may type to Siri and switch between text and speech to speak with her in whatever manner seems suitable at the moment.
Customers can now access hundreds of FAQs about using the iPhone, iPad, and Mac, as well as device help wherever they are using Siri. Users can ask questions about everything from scheduling an email in the Mail app to switching from Light to Dark Mode.

When a user asks Siri about scheduling text messages on the iPhone 15 Pro, Siri answers.
With onscreen awareness, Siri makes it easy to do an action linked to data on the screen, such adding an address from Messages to a friend's contact card. Siri will eventually be able to understand user content when more apps become aware of the screen. For example, if a buddy texts you about

their new address via Messages, you can reply, "Add this address to his contact card."

- **<u>Using Siri to Add an Address on a Contact Card</u>**

With Siri, you can now do hundreds of new things both within and between apps. For example, you may use Messages and Mail to obtain book recommendations from pals.

Thanks to Apple Intelligence, Siri will be able to do hundreds more actions in both Apple and third-party apps. For example, you may ask Siri to "Bring up that article about cicadas from my Reading List" or "Send the photos from the Saturday barbecue to Malia."

Siri searches friends' book recommendations for users of the iPhone 15 Pro.

With Siri, you can now do hundreds of new things both within and between apps. For example, you may use Messages and Mail to obtain book recommendations from pals.

Saying, "Play that podcast that Jamie recommended," for example, will cause Siri to locate and play the episode, saving the user from having to remember if it was mentioned in an email or text. Alternatively, they can ask, "What time does Mom's flight arrive? "With the aid of user-specific on-device data, Siri will be able to provide insight.", and Siri will obtain the flight details and provide an approximate arrival time by comparing them with the current flight monitoring.

- **Siri's Data-Driven On-Device Intelligence**

Based on the user's device information, Siri can offer individualized intelligence for tasks like remembering a dinner reservation or obtaining information about an upcoming flight.

Chapter Seven: Privacy in AI

Apple Intelligence sets a new standard for privacy in AI with on-device processing and Private Cloud Compute, which extends the security and privacy of Apple products into the cloud.

- ## An Innovative AI Privacy Framework

On-device processing is a fundamental component of Apple Intelligence, and many of the models that power it are fully on-device. Private Cloud Compute extends the security and privacy of Apple devices into the cloud to unleash even more intelligence by enabling the execution of more complex requests that demand more processing power. To be truly helpful, Apple Intelligence must protect user privacy while comprehending profound personal context.

With Private Cloud Compute, Apple Intelligence can expand and scale its processing capacity by utilizing larger, server-based models for more sophisticated queries. These models are based on Apple silicon and operate on servers, providing Apple with the infrastructure to ensure that data is never preserved or made public.

Private Cloud Compute cryptographically ensures that an iPhone, iPad, or Mac won't connect with a server unless its software has been made publicly available for review. By empowering users to access trustworthy intelligence, Apple Intelligence with Private Cloud Compute sets a new standard for privacy in AI. The code running on Apple silicon servers may be examined by independent specialists to confirm privacy.

Chapter Eight: ChatGPT Integration

To enable customers to take advantage of ChatGPT's expertise without having to jump between apps, Apple is integrating ChatGPT access into the iOS 18, iPadOS 18, and macOS Sequoia experiences.

- ## An Integration of ChatGPT Across the Apple Product Line

To enable customers to take advantage of ChatGPT's expertise and its capacity to understand documents and images without having to jump between apps, Apple is integrating ChatGPT access into the iOS 18, iPadOS 18, and macOS Sequoia experiences.

Siri can leverage ChatGPT's experience as needed. Users are alerted before transmitting any documents, photos, or questions to ChatGPT; after that, Siri gives the answer directly.

Say this to Siri on an iPhone 15 Pro: "I have fresh salmon, lemons, tomatoes." Help me prepare a five-course meal that will satisfy everyone's palate.

When an iPhone 15 Pro user asks Siri a question, she says, "Would you like me to use ChatGPT to do that?"

The results of ChatGPT are displayed using Siri on the iPhone 15 Pro. The first dish, bruschetta with tomatoes and basil, is described in bullet points.

With permission, Siri can leverage ChatGPT's vast knowledge library to provide an answer directly to the user.

Additionally, ChatGPT will be available via Apple's system-wide Writing Tools, which help users generate content for any type of writing.

Composed users can also use ChatGPT's picture capabilities to produce images in a variety of styles to complement their writing.

Using Pages' Compose function, a user provides a prompt about writing a bedtime story about Annie, a 6-year-old who loves to solve riddles.

A user uses Pages' Compose tool to access ChatGPT picture tools. The menu provides a number of suggested themes, including "Include a backstory for the caterpillar," "Add a magical impressionist image," and "Add a photorealistic image of the story."

Pages shows a bedtime story with a picture that the user produced in Compose.

ChatGPT users enjoy integrated privacy protections including disguised IP addresses and no request storing by OpenAI. ChatGPT's data-use policies apply to users who choose to link their accounts.

Later this year, ChatGPT—which leverages GPT-4o—will be accessible for iOS 18, iPadOS 18, and macOS Sequoia. Users can access it without having to register for a free account, and subscribers can link their accounts to take advantage of premium features straight from these interactions.

Conclusion

Imagine having a conversation with a genius who can answer any question, provide insights, and even generate text. Welcome to the world of ChatGPT, a revolutionary AI model that's changing the way we interact with technology. Apple Intelligence takes it to the next level by integrating ChatGPT into its ecosystem, making it easily accessible across all Apple devices.

ChatGPT is more than just a chatbot - it's a knowledge powerhouse. This AI model has been trained on a vast amount of text data, allowing it to understand context, nuances, and subtleties of human language. With ChatGPT, you can ask questions, seek advice, and even generate text. The possibilities are endless.

Imagine you're a student working on a research project. You can ask ChatGPT to provide information on a specific topic, and it will respond with accurate and relevant data. You can even ask it to summarize a lengthy article or generate a thesis statement.

ChatGPT is not just limited to information retrieval. It can also generate text based on your prompts. Want to write a story but struggling with writer's block? ChatGPT can help you generate ideas, plotlines, and even entire paragraphs.

The integration of ChatGPT into Apple Intelligence takes conversational AI to new heights. With the ability to access ChatGPT across all Apple devices, you can harness the power of AI anywhere, anytime.

Imagine being able to ask Siri or your Apple Watch to summarize a news article or generate a response to an email. With ChatGPT integration, this is now possible.

In addition to its conversational capabilities, ChatGPT can also generate images based on your prompts. Want to create a unique image for a social media post? ChatGPT can help you generate it.

The possibilities with ChatGPT integration are endless. Whether you're a student, professional, or simply someone who wants to explore the world of AI, Apple Intelligence has made it easy and accessible.

In conclusion, the integration of ChatGPT into Apple Intelligence marks a significant milestone in the world of AI. With its conversational capabilities, text generation, and image creation, ChatGPT is revolutionizing the way we interact with technology. As we continue to navigate the digital landscape, it's clear that AI will play a significant role in shaping our future. Apple Intelligence is at the forefront of this revolution, empowering users to harness the power of AI like never before.

www.ingramcontent.com/pod-product-compliance
Lightning Source LLC
Chambersburg PA
CBHW030044230526
45472CB00005B/1660